History Makers

Anne Frank

... and her diary

Sarah Ridley

FRANKLIN WATTS

This edition 2013

First published in 2009 by
Franklin Watts
338 Euston Road
London NW1 3BH

Franklin Watts Australia
Level 17/207 Kent Street
Sydney NSW 2000

Series Editor: Jeremy Smith
Art Director: Jonathan Hair
Design: Simon Morse
Cover Design: Jonathan Hair
Picture Research: Sarah Ridley

Picture credits: Anne Frank House/
Getty Images: 5, 6, 9, 13, 20, 22.
AKG Images: front cover left, 7.
Hulton Archive/Getty Images: 12, 17.
Longhurst/Topfoto: 15.
Picturepoint/Topham: 23.
Roger-Viollet/Getty Images: 21.
Michael Teller/AKG Images:19.
Three Lions/Hulton Archive/Getty
Images: 18. Ullstein Bild/ AKG Images:
front cover right, 1, 10, 11, 14. George W
Wales/Hulton Archive/Getty Images: 8.

Dewey classification: 940.53
ISBN: 978 1 4451 1791 1

A CIP catalogue record for this book is available
from the British Library

Franklin Watts is a division of Hachette Children's
Books, an Hachette UK company.
www.hachette.co.uk

Printed in China

Contents

The Frank family

On 12 June 1929, Anne Frank was born in Germany.
Her parents already had a daughter called Margot.
The family was Jewish and had many friends, both Jews and Christians.

Margot (left) and Anne (right) with their father, Otto Frank, in 1930.

Edith and Otto Frank marry.

Margot Frank is born.

Anne Frank is born.

Worldwide money crisis.

Early life

As a small child, Anne played in the garden and on the street.

Anne liked to play in the sandpit. Here her mother stands close by.

1930s

Support for the Nazi Party grows.

January
1933

Hitler and the Nazi Party take power in Germany.

Adolf Hitler salutes some German soldiers.

Anne's parents began to worry about the new leader of Germany, Adolf Hitler. Hitler and the Nazi Party wanted to rid Germany of Jews and other people whom they did not see as German.

March
1933

The Nazi Party starts to send people to concentration camps.

April
1933

The Nazi Party begins to make laws against Jews.

The Franks in Amsterdam

Like many Jewish families, the Franks no longer felt safe in Germany. They moved to Amsterdam in the Netherlands in 1934.

The parents of these Jewish children sent them to safety in England.

1930s ▶

Thousands of Jews leave Germany.

1934 ▶

The Franks move to the Netherlands.

Anne and Margot soon felt at home in their new flat. They made some friends, went to school, took gym lessons and went on day trips to the seaside.

Anne's father liked to take photographs. This one shows Anne (second from left) and her friends on her 10th birthday.

1938 ▶

The Germans take over Austria and parts of Czechoslovakia.

June
1939 ▶

Anne's 10th birthday.

The Second World War

The German army marched into the Netherlands in 1940.

In 1939, Germany invaded Poland. England and France declared war on Germany. Then the German army invaded the Netherlands.

1939	April 1940	June 1940
The Second World War begins.	The German army invades the Netherlands.	France surrenders.

▲ Anne worked hard at school.

At first Anne's life stayed much the same. She went to school, did her homework and played with her friends.

June
1940 ▶

Anne's 11th birthday.

December
1940 ▶

Otto Frank's business moves to
263 Prinsengracht, Amsterdam.

11

Jews under attack

But life began to change. Jewish children had to go to Jewish schools. Jews were not allowed to travel by tram, bus or car. Many lost their jobs.

All Jews over the age of six had to wear a yellow star with 'Jew' written on it.

April
1941 ▶
The Germans give out identity cards to all Dutch people.

December
1941 ▶
The USA joins the war, fighting on Britain's side.

In June 1942 Anne's parents gave her a diary for her 13th birthday. She decided to write to the diary as if it were a friend called Kitty.

Anne's diary. She began each entry, 'Dear Kitty'.

1942 ▶

The Germans make laws about what Dutch Jews may or may not do.

June
1942 ▶

Anne's 13th birthday.

13

The Secret Annex

Anne's father prepared a hiding place for the family. He was afraid that the Germans would send them to concentration camps.

This photo shows Anne not long before she went into hiding.

29 June
1942 ▶

The Germans state that all Dutch Jews will be sent to camps in Germany.

When Anne's sister, Margot, was ordered to enter a camp, the family had to act. They fled their flat and moved into the hiding place, called the Secret Annex.

◀ The Secret Annex was above and behind Otto Frank's office and storeroom. The building is now a museum.

6 July
1942 ▶
The Frank family goes into hiding.

1942 ▶
Battles are fought around the world.

Life in the Secret Annex

Peter van Pel's room

It was a shock for Anne to live in such a small space. Soon the van Pels family and a dentist, called Mr Pfeffer, joined them.

Otto, Edith and Margot Frank's room

Anne had to share a room with Mr Pfeffer

This drawing shows the rooms in the Secret Annex.

13 July 1942 ▶	November 1942 ▶
The van Pels family enters the Secret Annex.	Mr Pfeffer joins the people hiding in the Secret Annex.

Many Jews went into hiding in the Netherlands, like these people who lived under the floorboards of a house.

Anne wrote in her diary saying how much she missed her friends, her freedom and her cat. Still, she knew that she was lucky to be safe.

1942 ▶

Thousands of Jewish prisoners are dying in concentration camps.

The helpers

Four workers at Otto's business agreed to bring food, books and clothes to the Secret Annex. They risked their own lives by doing this.

During the war, people often had to queue for food all across Europe. These people are on a French street.

1942 ▶

Food shortages and food rationing.

1942 ▶

The war continues with battles on land, in the air and at sea.

During office hours, the Frank family and their friends had to be very quiet in case anyone heard them. They could not run the tap or flush the toilet.

The helpers built a bookcase in front of the stairs to the Secret Annex, to hide it from the other workers.

June
1943

July
1943

Anne's 14th birthday.

There is a burglary in the offices below the Secret Annex.

Anne's secret life

Anne recorded her friendship with Peter van Pels, shown here.

Anne wrote about everyday life in her diary. She kept busy by reading, doing schoolwork, learning new skills and helping out. She hoped to be a writer after the war.

1943 ▶
The war is not going as well for Germany.

1944 ▶
Anne's friendship with Peter develops.

April
1944 ▶
Another burglary in the offices downstairs.

German soldiers gather up Polish Jews to send them to concentration camps.

In her diary, Anne described how scared she was of being discovered. Sadly, her fears came true.

June
1944 ▶

The British and other forces invade Normandy in France.

June
1944 ▶

Anne's 15th birthday.

Discovery!

On 4 August 1944, men stormed into the Secret Annex. They sent everyone to concentration camps. Anne Frank died in a concentration camp in 1945, like six million other Jews. Out of the people who had lived in the Secret Annex, only Anne's father, Otto Frank (right), survived.

4 August 1944 ▶	4 September 1944 ▶	October 1944 ▶
Police enter the Secret Annex.	The inhabitants are sent to concentration camps.	Margot and Anne enter the Bergen-Belsen camp

After the war, Otto discovered that one of the helpers had kept Anne's diary. He decided that other people should read Anne's words and the diary was published in 1947.

Anne's diary. Millions of people have read it worldwide.

February/March **1945**	May **1945**	**1947**
Margot and Anne die.	The Second World War ends in Europe.	*The Diary of Anne Frank* is published.

Glossary

Concentration camp A prison camp. The Germans sent Jews and others to concentration camps, where millions of people lived and died in horrible conditions.

Hitler Adolf Hitler was the leader of the Nazi Party in Germany.

Identity card A card that states a person's name, age and maybe religion. The Germans used identity cards to find Jews more easily.

Invasion When one country sends its army into another country.

Jew Someone of the Jewish race or religion.

Laws Rules made by a government.

Nazi Party The National Socialist Party founded by Adolf Hitler.

Rationing Restricting the amount of food or goods to make sure there is enough for everybody.

Index